D0906104

A+ books are published by Capstone Press,
1710 Roe Crest Drive, North Mankato, Minnesota 56003.
www.capstonepub.com

Books published by Capstone Press are manufactured with paper
containing at least 10 percent post-consumer waste.

Library of Congress Cataloging-in-Publication Data
McCurry, Kristen.
  Up-close mysteries : zoomed-in photo puzzles / by Kristen McCurry.
     p. cm.—(A+ books. Eye-look picture games)
  Includes bibliographical references.
  Summary: "Simple text invites readers to guess the subject of the photo based on a few
zoomed-in views"—Provided by publisher.
  ISBN 978-1-4296-7550-5 (library binding)
  1. Picture puzzles—Juvenile literature. I. Title.
  GV1507.P47M378 2012
  793.73—dc23   2011043261

Credits

Jeni Wittrock, editor; Tracy Davies McCabe, designer; Marcie Spence, media researcher; Laura
Manthe, production specialist; Sarah Schuette, photo stylist; Marcy Morin, studio scheduler

Photo Credits

Capstone Studio: Karon Dubke, 4 (left), 11, 12, 13, 14; iStockphoto: abalcazar, 29, 30, christianl,
19, 20, hammondovi, 21, 22, iofoto, 3 (middle), 4 (right), 17, 18; Shutterstock: Dmitry Kalinovsky,
15, 16, Evan Meyer, 5, 6, Isantilli, 3 (left), 7, 8, Johan Swanepoel, 9, 10, Natalia Barsukova, 25, 26,
Peteri, 23, 24, Rich Carey, cover, Richard Paul Kane, 3 (right), 27, 28, Tom Wang, 31

Note to Parents, Teachers, and Librarians

The Eye-Look Picture Games series supports national math standards related to grouping and
sorting and national language arts standards related to the use of comparisons and analogies.
The images support early readers in understanding the text. The repetition of words and phrases
helps early readers learn new words. Early readers may need assistance to read some words and
to use the Read More and Internet Sites sections of the book.

Printed in the United States of America in North Mankato, Minnesota.
102011   006405CGS12

Table of Contents

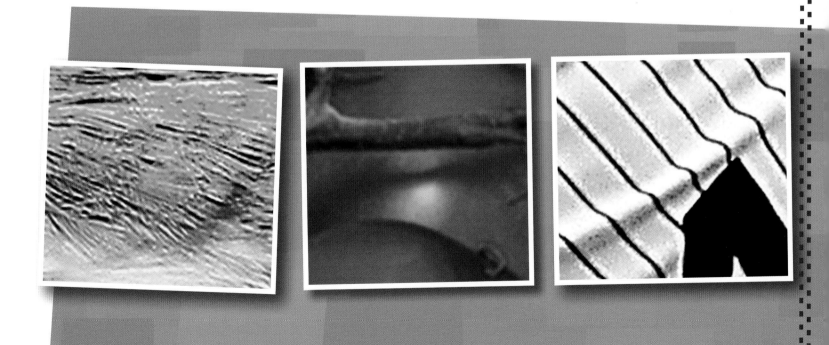

Have you ever looked at something really, really close-up? It's called "zooming in." Find something close by and try it! Zoom in on a banana, a pencil, your hand—anything!

Does it look different? Do you see things you haven't noticed before? Does it even look like the same object?

This book lets you zoom in on all sorts of things. You'll see four different parts of one picture very close-up. It's like a puzzle you have to put together. Can you guess what you're seeing? Turn each page to find out!

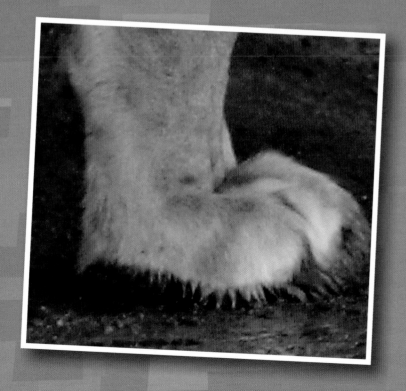

It's a lion!

mane

eye

tail

paw

This king of the African savanna uses its big **paws** to chase and bring down prey.

Lions are the only member of the cat family with **manes**.

A lion's **eyes** can see five times better than human eyes can.

Only lions have dark tufts at the ends of their **tails**. They use them to communicate with other lions.

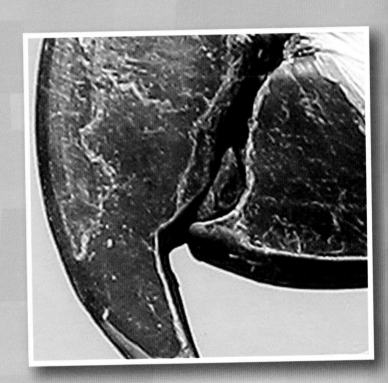

eye

beak

feathers

claw

It's a macaw!

The macaw, a type of parrot, uses its large, pointed **beak** to crack nuts and seeds.

The curved **claws** on a macaw's foot help the bird grip branches.

A macaw's brightly colored **feathers** help it blend in with the colorful fruits and flowers of the South American rain forest.

Most macaws have dark **eyes** as babies. As they grow, their eyes change from black to gray to white to yellow.

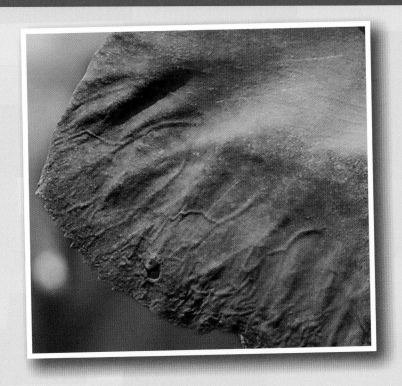

ear

tusk

trunk

foot

It's an elephant!

An elephant's **trunk** is a long nose used for smelling, grabbing, drinking, trumpeting, and even snorkeling!

Elephants have ivory **tusks** that help them dig for food such as roots or tree bark.

Elephants use their large **ears** to fan themselves in the hot African sun.

Wide, padded **feet** allow elephants to walk softly through the forests and savannas.

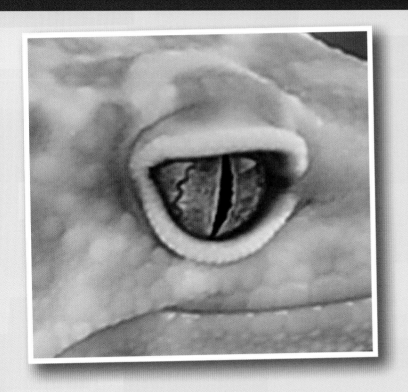

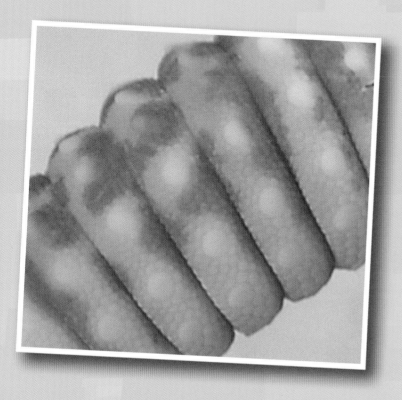

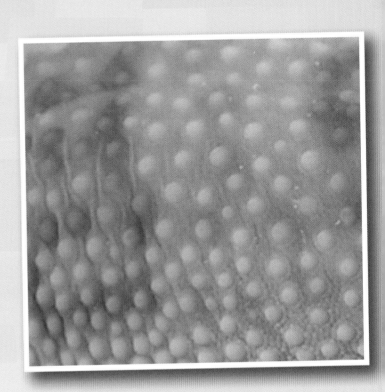

It's a gecko!

eye

skin

toes

tail

A gecko's knobby **skin** blends in with its surroundings.

Some geckos have special pads on their fingers and **toes** that allow them to climb walls and even walk on ceilings!

If a predator grabs a gecko's **tail**, the tail may fall off so the gecko can escape.

Most geckos don't have **eyes** with movable lids. They have a clear eyelid that they clean with their tongues.

flashing lights

windshield wipers

stop sign

wheel

It's a school bus!

A school bus has red and yellow **lights** that flash as the bus is stopping to let children on or off.

When the **stop sign** swings out, other drivers know to stop and watch for children.

A school bus has giant **windshield wipers** so the driver can see on rainy days.

There are four **wheels** on a school bus, which carry the weight of the bus—about 30,000 pounds (13,608 kilograms)!

hard hat

safety harness

work boots

concrete

It's construction work!

Workers wear **hard hats** to protect their heads on the job site.

Safety harnesses are special belts that keep workers from falling, especially when they're up high.

Many **work boots** are steel toed. They have a steel shell inside that protects the toes in case something gets dropped on them.

Workers use lots of **concrete** to build things. It's made of cement, sand, pebbles, and water.

list

grocery cart

sign

pineapple

It's a grocery store!

Shoppers use **grocery carts**, or baskets, to carry lots of groceries.

Signs show the price of food. These tomatoes cost $3.49 per pound.

People often bring a **grocery list** to the store to help them remember what they need to buy.

You can buy fresh vegetables and fruit like this **pineapple** in the produce section.

chef hat

oven

It's a pizza place!

pizza box

toppings

Pizzas to go come in large, flat, cardboard **boxes**.

Big **ovens** with shelves are used to cook many pizzas at once.

Pizzas come with all kinds of different **toppings**, including meat, vegetables, and even little fish called anchovies.

Many pizza cooks wear **chef hats** as part of their uniform. It makes them look professional and keeps their hair out of the food.

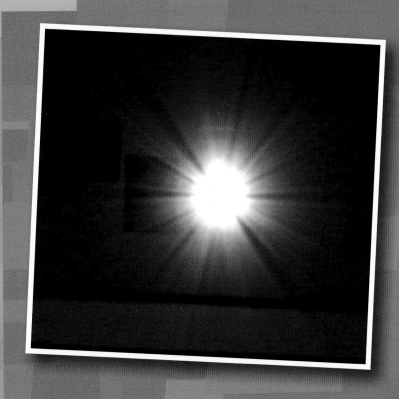

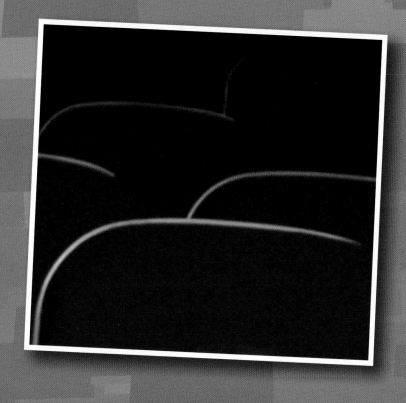

It's a movie theater!

That shiny light is the **projector**, shining the movie up onto the screen.

Most theaters have **seats** that flip down when they're being used.

Concession stands at movie theaters have been selling **popcorn** since the 1930s!

Three-dimensional (3-D) movies require special **glasses**. These movies look like they are coming out of the screen!

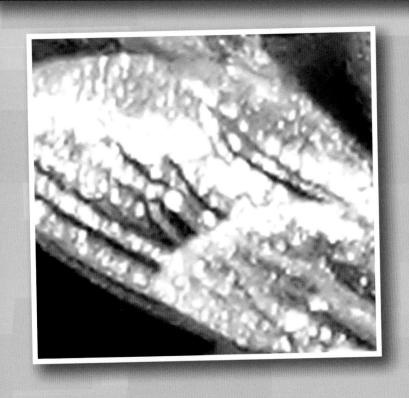

cell

wing

eyes

body

It's a beehive!

Honeybees have five **eyes**—three small ones on top and two big ones in front.

Bzzz! The fast movement of the honeybee's **wings** is what makes their buzzing sound.

Honeybee **bodies** are yellow and black. The boldly colored stripes warn other animals to stay away.

Each honeycomb **cell** is a hexagon, which is a six-sided shape.

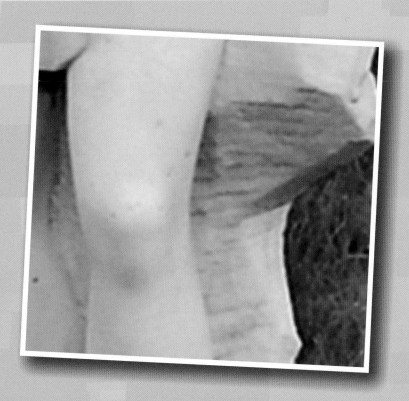

tree

statue

sidewalk

flowers

It's a park!

Some parks have **statues** as decorations or to celebrate famous people.

Gardeners work hard to keep parks beautiful with plants and **flowers**.

There are **sidewalks** or trails in many parks for walking or biking.

Trees make homes for animals, and they make shade for people at the park.

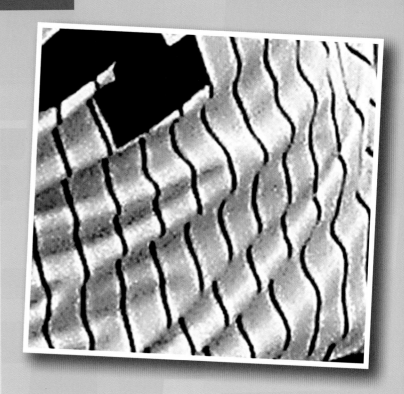

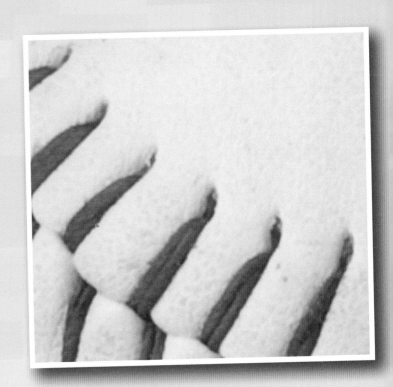

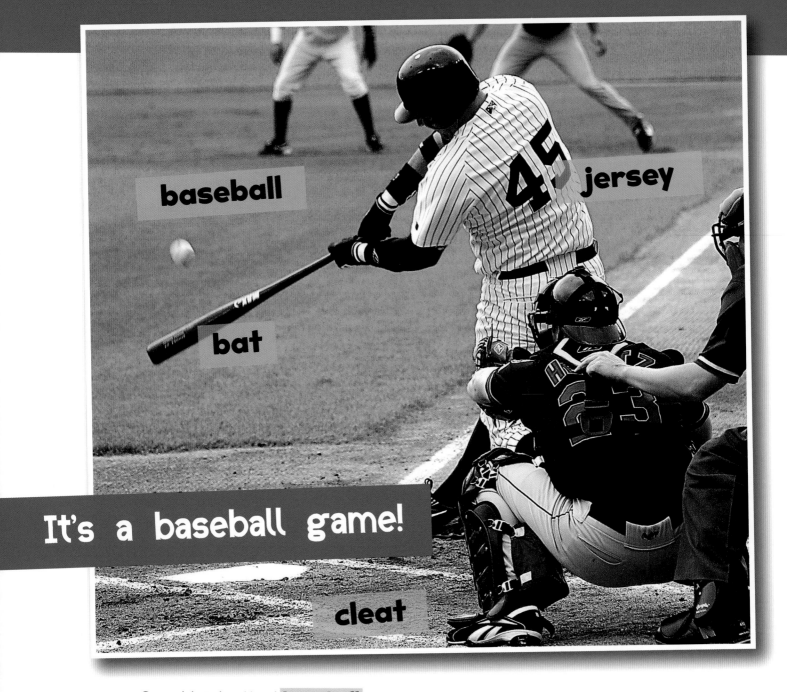

baseball

jersey

bat

cleat

It's a baseball game!

Crack! A batted **baseball** can travel more than 100 miles (161 kilometers) per hour!

Most baseball **bats** are made of wood or aluminum.

Cleats are shoes with plastic, rubber, or metal prongs on the bottom. They keep athletes from slipping and help them go faster.

A baseball **jersey** is the shirt a player wears. Every jersey has a number.

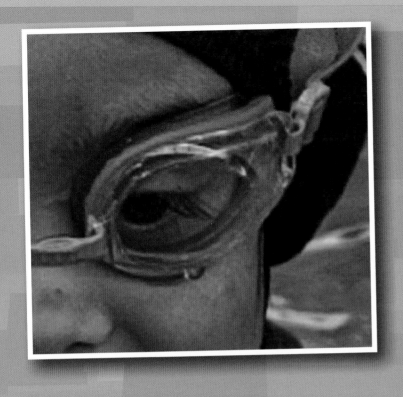

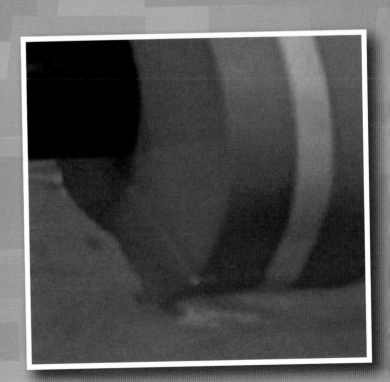

swim cap

goggles

floating barbells

waves

It's a swimmer!

Goggles help you see underwater and keep splashes out of your eyes.

It's a good idea to wear a **swim cap** to keep your hair out of your face and keep the pool clean.

All the kicking and splashing from swimmers cause lots of **waves**.

Floating barbells help people stay above water while they're learning to swim.

How did you do? Did you know what the up-close pictures were? Were you able to guess what the pieces of the puzzle showed?

Looking at something close up lets you see it in a whole new way. Try using a magnifying glass to zoom in on all kinds of things. You might be surprised at what you see.

Read More

Peterson, Megan Cooley. *Camouflage Clues: A Photo Riddle Book.* Nature Riddles. Mankato, Minn.: Capstone Press, 2010.

Chedru, Delphine. *Spot It! Find the Hidden Creatures.* New York: Abrams Books for Young Readers, 2009.

Marzollo, Jean. *I Spy an Egg in a Nest.* I Spy Books. New York: Scholastic, 2011.

Internet Sites

FactHound offers a safe, fun way to find Internet sites related to this book. All of the sites on FactHound have been researched by our staff.

Here's all you do:

Visit www.facthound.com

Type in this code: 9781429675505

Super-cool stuff!

Check out projects, games and lots more at
www.capstonekids.com